# SUCCEEDING AS A
SELF-MANAGED TEAM

A Practical Guide To Operating As A Self-Managed Work Team

Richard Y. Chang

Mark J. Curtin

Richard Chang Associates, Inc.
Publications Division
Irvine, California

SUCCEEDING AS A SELF-MANAGED TEAM

A Practical Guide To Operating As A
Self-Managed Work Team

Richard Y. Chang
Mark J. Curtin

Library of Congress Catalog Card Number
93-91040

© 1994, Richard Chang Associates, Inc.
Printed in the United States of America

ISBN 1-883553-20-2

Third printing April 1995

Richard Chang Associates, Inc.
Publications Division
41 Corporate Park, Suite 230
Irvine, CA 92714
(800) 756-8096 • Fax (714) 756-0853

RICHARD
CHANG
ASSOCIATES

ACKNOWLEDGMENTS

About The Authors

Richard Y. Chang is President and CEO of Richard Chang Associates, Inc., a diversified, organizational improvement consulting firm based in Irvine, California. He is internationally recognized for his expertise in management strategy, quality improvement, organization development, customer satisfaction, and human resource development.

Mark J. Curtin, is the Principal Consultant and founder of Effectiveness Plus⁺, a training and consulting firm based in Ventura County, California. His expertise includes quality/process improvement, performance management, leadership development and organizational learning.

The authors would like to acknowledge the support of the entire team of professionals at Richard Chang Associates, Inc. for their contribution to the guidebook development process. In addition, special thanks are extended to the many client organizations who have helped us shape the practical ideas and proven methods shared in this guidebook.

Additional Credits

Reviewers:	Jim Greeley and P. Keith Kelly
Editor:	Sarah Ortlieb Fraser
Graphic Layout:	Jackie Westfall, Doug Westfall Suzanne Jamieson, and Christina Slater
Cover Design:	John Odam Design Associates

TRANSITION TEAM
CROSS-TRAINING PLAN WORKSHEET

TEAM MEMBER	CURRENT JOB	PARTNER	CROSS-TRAINED JOB	TEAM

ACTION PLAN WORKSHEET

ACTION STEP TASK/ACTIVITY	RESPONSIBLE PERSONS/GROUP	BEGIN DATE	END DATE	ESTIMATED HOURS	COST
1.					
2.					
3.					
4.					
5.					
6.					
7.					
8.					

THE PRACTICAL GUIDEBOOK COLLECTION
FROM RICHARD CHANG ASSOCIATES, INC.
PUBLICATIONS DIVISION

Our Practical Guidebook Collection is growing to meet the challenges of the ever-changing workplace of the 90's. Look for these and other titles from Richard Chang Associates, Inc. on your bookstore shelves and in book catalogs.

QUALITY IMPROVEMENT SERIES

- Meetings That Work!
- Continuous Improvement Tools Volume 1
- Continuous Improvement Tools Volume 2
- Step-By-Step Problem Solving
- Satisfying Internal Customers First!
- Continuous Process Improvement
- Improving Through Benchmarking
- Succeeding As A Self-Managed Team
- Process Reengineering In Action

MANAGEMENT SKILLS SERIES

- Coaching Through Effective Feedback
- Expanding Leadership Impact
- Mastering Change Management
- On-The-Job Orientation And Training
- Re-Creating Teams During Transitions

HIGH PERFORMANCE TEAM SERIES

- Success Through Teamwork
- Team Decision-Making Techniques
- Measuring Team Performance
- Building A Dynamic Team

HIGH-IMPACT TRAINING SERIES

- Creating High-Impact Training
- Identifying Targeted Training Needs
- Mapping A Winning Training Approach
- Producing High-Impact Learning Tools
- Applying Successful Training Techniques
- Measuring The Impact Of Training
- Make Your Training Results Last

PREFACE

The 1990's have already presented individuals and organizations with some very difficult challenges to face and overcome. So who will have the advantage as we move toward the year 2000 and beyond?

The advantage will belong to those with a commitment to continuous learning. Whether on an individual basis or as an entire organization, one key ingredient to building a continuous learning environment is *The Practical Guidebook Collection* brought to you by the Publications Division of Richard Chang Associates, Inc.

After understanding the future *"learning needs"* expressed by our clients and other potential customers, we are pleased to publish *The Practical Guidebook Collection*. These guidebooks are designed to provide you with proven, *"real-world"* tips, tools, and techniques on a wide range of subjects that you can apply in the workplace and/or on a personal level immediately!

Once you've had a chance to benefit from *The Practical Guidebook Collection*, please feel free to share your feedback with us. Your feedback is so important that we've included a brief *Evaluation and Feedback Form* at the end of the guidebook that you may fax to us at (714) 756-0853.

With your feedback, we can continuously improve the resources we are providing through the Publications Division of Richard Chang Associates, Inc.

Wishing you successful reading,

Richard Y. Chang
President and CEO
Richard Chang Associates, Inc.

TABLE OF CONTENTS

"World's greatest management principle: you can work miracles by having faith in others. To get the best of our people, choose to think and believe the best about them."

Anonymous

CHAPTER ONE

INTRODUCTION

Why Read This Guidebook?

Making the transition from a traditionally managed department or work group to a self-managed team is not an easy task. It requires people to work together differently, deal with sensitive issues they did not have to deal with before, and handle problems that were previously managed by others. The transition itself can be quite a challenge—one that some groups succeed at, while others don't.

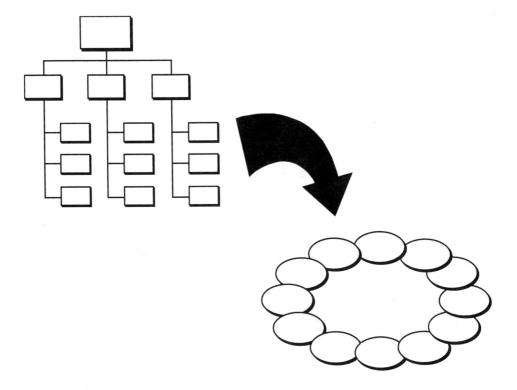

This guidebook presents a solid foundation for groups looking to plan, organize, and implement the transition to self-managed teams. It provides an outline of what to expect during the transition, and does so in a logical, sequential, and straight-forward manner.

Who Should Read This Guidebook?

If you are a member of a self-managed team or are considering the transition from a traditionally managed group, then this book will prepare you for what's ahead.

If you are joining a team that is already self-managing, then this guidebook will provide a good idea of what to expect as part of your new team.

Self-managed teams are becoming widespread in all industries and all levels of organizations. Whether you are in sales, engineering, management, production, or in a small business, the tools and techniques that follow will be valuable for you and your team.

When And How To Use It

Use this book as a guide when making the transition to a self-managed team. Team members can use it to plan what needs to be done in each phase of the transition by reviewing this guidebook before each planning session.

It can also be used in a workshop or training setting to prepare all team members for the transition.

Established self-managed teams will find it valuable too, as a means of evaluating their ongoing progress and as a tool to ensure the team continues to flourish.

Appendix A contains brief summaries of challenges faced by self-managed teams on an ongoing basis. It focuses on the skills necessary to respond to these challenges. You and your team can use the points covered there as mini case studies to examine your team's abilities and competencies in these areas.

WHAT ARE SELF-MANAGED TEAMS?

A new approach to managing work activities, which does not rely on a supervisor or management making all decisions, is *"self-managed teams."* A self-managed team differs from a traditional work group by taking full advantage of all team members' talents, skills, abilities, ideas, and experiences.

In traditional work groups, members often do not have the opportunity to express their ideas because management usually makes the decisions *(even if members know a better way to get the job done).*

Although traditional work groups can be highly effective with the right dynamics, in reality there are often limitations. For example, in most organizations, supervisors make key decisions for the work group. This approach can limit work group performance for two reasons:

> ☞ It doesn't make full use of each group member's talent, experience, knowledge, common sense, and
>
> ☞ It doesn't encourage teamwork.

This can be both wasteful and ineffective. It wastes the brainpower, experience, abilities, and practical knowledge of those who actually produce and deliver the organization's products and services.

People with the ability to perform numerous jobs often just do the same job, year after year, without ever having the chance to learn new skills. Those with many years of experience cannot contribute fully to the success of the organization because their jobs only draw upon some of their talents.

When successfully implemented, self-managed teams have proven to be more effective than traditional work groups because they truly create teamwork. Most work groups do not operate like teams because each person is only responsible for their part of the job. In a self-managed team, if one person fails, the whole team suffers. Teamwork becomes a priority. Team members learn to hold each other accountable for doing whatever it takes to get the job done.

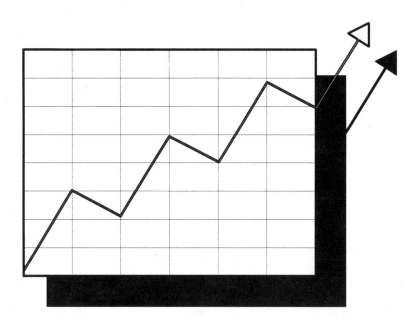

A variety of changes in team member roles and responsibilities occur when shifting from a traditional work group to a self-managed team. Some of these changes include:

	SUPERVISOR (TRADITIONAL)	TEAM MEMBERS (SELF-MANAGED)
RESPONSIBILITIES OF TRADITIONAL WORK GROUPS VERSUS SELF-MANAGED TEAMS		
Is responsible for schedules, assignments, budgets, hiring, reviews, etc.	X	X
Makes key decisions	X	X
Reports directly to upper management	X	X
Coordinates with other groups	X	X
Is accountable for quality of work group's results	X	X

As you can see, self-managed teams are quite different from traditional work groups. Employees need to learn new skills (*or use existing skills differently*) to succeed as members of a self-managed team. These skills involve performing multiple work assignments. They also involve new ways of interacting with each other and with people outside the team.

The skills that contribute to the success of a self-managed team are:

⇒ Leadership

⇒ Communication

⇒ Process improvement

⇒ Team dynamics

⇒ Project management

⇒ Conflict management

⇒ Consensus decision making

⇒ Peer coaching and feedback

⇒ Group problem solving

⇒ Interpersonal

1

2

3

4

5

6

Note: These skills are covered in depth in Appendix A.

Team members must also have certain individual abilities. However, these abilities are not job skills because they are often subjective and emotional in nature. They are personal decisions and choices. They include a willingness to:

→ accept change

→ try new things

→ take on more responsibility

→ be held accountable for results

→ take action, instead of waiting to be told what to do

→ act in the best interests of the team rather than oneself

→ work responsibly without the need for supervision

→ help other team members succeed

→ take risks

→ be open-minded

Benefits Of Self-Managed Teams

As you can see, there are many transitions and changes that a work group, and its individual members, must face on the road to becoming a fully functioning, self-managed team.

On the other hand, there are many benefits to being a self-managed team. On the following pages, you will gain a greater understanding of:

➠ What's in it for you?

➠ What's in it for your organization?

➠ What's in it for your customers?

Once you've explored some of the potential benefits, you can determine which benefits you and/or your work team would like to experience.

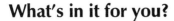

What's in it for you?

Why should you support this change to self-managed teams? Will your life at work be easier or more enjoyable? Self-managed teams offer many benefits to you, your organization, and to your customers. The benefits include:

Greater job variety

Self-managed team members do not do the same thing every day. You can rotate roles, perhaps a few times a day. This makes your daily work more interesting.

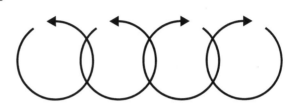

More freedom to make the right decisions and act on them

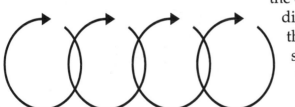

Before you were a member of a self-managed team, your supervisor made all the decisions. You may have disagreed with some of them. As a member of a self-managed team, you will participate in all decisions.

Increased opportunities to learn new skills

The more skills you have, the more valuable you will be to your employer and all future employers. Learning new abilities often leads to pay increases. Traditional work groups typically do not offer the opportunity to learn as many new skills in so little time.

What's in it for your organization?

Some of the benefits your organization will experience after implementing self-managed teams include:

Increased employee commitment to decisions

People are more likely to see a project through to success when they help choose the direction. When employees are *assigned* to do something, they may care less about getting the job done. When you personally make a commitment to a customer, the urgency of the job will be more real to you.

Greater work team productivity

The quality of work is much better. More work is completed on time, and the pace of work may even increase. When work groups are more involved with deciding how the work gets done, they tend to approach work assignments with more enthusiasm. This trait often results in greater team productivity.

More operational flexibility

Members of self-managed teams tend to learn more about each other's job responsibilities because the team is collectively responsible for achieving results. When someone calls in sick, it's typically less of a problem since everyone is multiskilled and can cover that position easily.

Improved levels of accountability

Finger pointing, excuses, and blaming others for problems decrease as the team becomes responsible for results. Without a long chain of command, it's easy to know who is responsible for what.

What's in it for your customers?

The biggest winner in the move to self-managed teams will be your customers, and satisfied customers are the key to the long-term survival of your organization. Some of the benefits your customers will experience include:

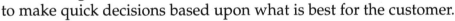

Quicker response times

Since decisions are made directly by those who produce products and deliver services, they can be made faster. No more waiting for approval from management. The team is able to make quick decisions based upon what is best for the customer.

Improved quality

Team members are able to truly focus on issues as a team, making it easier to reach a consensus on the critical issue of meeting and exceeding customers' quality expectations.

Direct customer contact

Your customers no longer have to figure out who to contact when they have a problem. They can go directly to the people who are doing the work for them. Fewer channels also means clearer communication.

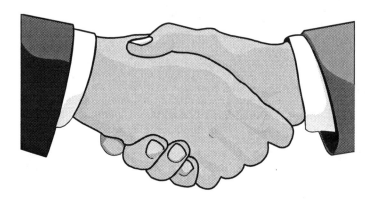

Faster delivery of products and services

The self-managed team has complete control over their work processes. This allows the team to reduce the time it takes to complete tasks. For example, the team may decide to reorder the tasks needed to produce their product or deliver their service. Wasted time or unnecessary tasks can be eliminated, so customers will receive their orders faster.

Everyone comes out a winner when an organization chooses self-managed teams because:

➡ Employees like having control over their work

➡ People are free to do what they know is best

➡ Work becomes more interesting and varied

➡ The organization gets a more empowered work force

➡ More work is done in less time

➡ Quality increases

➡ Turnaround time decreases, as do costs

All this leads to satisfied and loyal customers, who will continue to use your organization's products and services.

Challenges On The Road To Self-Managed Teams

Resistance to change

Many people are set in their ways and feel life would be much less complicated if things weren't changing all the time. It is the responsibility of fellow team members to encourage those having difficulty accepting changes to keep an open mind and be part of the solution, not the problem.

Avoidance of team coordinator role

Self-managed team members usually share the role of team coordinator. This role may rotate every eight to twelve weeks *(or more, depending on the nature of the team)*. The coordinator keeps upper management informed of the team's progress.

Some team members may be wary of this role, so it's the responsibility of fellow team members to encourage these people and to boost their self-confidence.

Fear of blame

Some people resist new responsibilities because they are afraid of being blamed if things go wrong. In self-managed teams, everybody shares responsibility for success or failure. Decisions are made by consensus. Mistakes are avoided if team members pitch in and help each other when needed.

Limited skills and abilities

No member of the self-managed team should be pushed beyond his limits. Everyone has different skills and abilities. Those who are able to learn every position on the team will have the opportunity to do any job. Others may only be capable of learning a few jobs, but should be encouraged to work up to their potential.

Distribution of pay

In some organizations, self-managed teams themselves decide how to distribute pay increase funds. If a team member believes that he will not receive a fair share of the increase, they discuss the issue during a team meeting. In addition, organizational policies may be a hurdle to the team managing this themselves.

Handling discipline issues

Supervisors have never enjoyed the job of disciplining an employee. It may not be easy for the team to confront a *"problem"* member, but since discipline issues have a strong impact on team dynamics and morale, the member must be dealt with.

Fear of the unknown

One of the advantages of the traditional work group is that it provides a sense of structure and certainty. It is a challenge for some people to let go of this and venture into the unknown realm of self-managed teams.

CHAPTER TWO WORKSHEET:
YOUR TRANSITION TO SELF-MANAGED TEAMS

1. What are the most important benefits you expect as part of a self-managed team?

_____

_____

_____

_____

2. What do you think your peers would describe as the most important benefits for them?

_____

_____

_____

_____

3. What benefits would there be for your organization?

_____

_____

_____

_____

4. How would your customers benefit?

_____

_____

_____

_____

_____

_____

5. What challenges do you foresee in transitioning to a self-managed team?

_____

_____

_____

_____

_____

_____

_____

_____

THE TEAM TRANSITION MODEL

Now that you understand what a self-managed team is, you can see it's not an easy change. The way you do work in your organization today is probably very different from how work is done in self-managed teams. You can't simply stop operating the way you are today, and begin working tomorrow as a self-managed team. It requires careful and thorough planning.

A good *"road map"* can help you change to a self-managed team environment. The transition model, which we will refer to as the PADIE model (Plan, Analyze, Design, Implement, and Evaluate), is just such a road map.

Let's look at what is involved in the five phases.

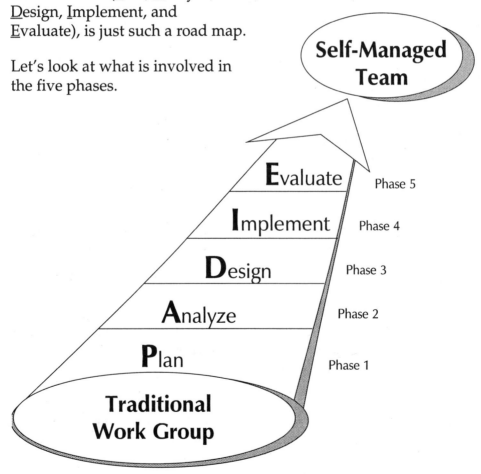

Self-Managed Team

Evaluate — Phase 5

Implement — Phase 4

Design — Phase 3

Analyze — Phase 2

Plan — Phase 1

Traditional Work Group

Plan

This first phase sets the stage by clarifying why you will be making the transition to a self-managed team. The team establishes its vision, mission, and values. It determines potential effects of transition on others in the organization and communicates issues and concerns to those affected.

Analyze

The team then analyzes its readiness by determining how it will handle its management responsibilities, its work responsibilities, and what cross-training is necessary.

Design

Designing the team involves assigning team-management responsibilities, designing the team's workflow, and setting ground rules for how team members will interact with each other and the organization.

Implement

The transition really gets underway when the team creates its first action plan as a self-managed team, implements the plan, monitors its progress, and improves its processes.

Evaluate

Team members provide feedback on each others' performance, and on the team's overall performance. In addition, evaluation feedback is obtained from outside the team.

The transition is not going to happen overnight. You can plan on taking nine to twelve months to proceed through the phases of the transition model. How long it takes will depend on your situation (*the size of the group, the organizational estimate, etc.*).

Prestige Printing: A Practical Example

Let's look at the case of Prestige Printing . . .

a company with 200 employees. Prestige recently decided to implement self-managed teams. The company chose its Prep Department to pilot the self-managed teams effort. Prestige plans to study the Prep Department's experiences before launching self-managed teams in all other departments.

Twenty-two people work in the Prep Department, which is organized into four groups according to the type of work they do *(film processing, stripping, proofing, and plate making).* Each of these groups has a supervisor, and members of each group are specialists in a particular skill.

Before the Prep Department is ready to operate as a self-managed team, they must first prepare for the changeover. Prestige decides to use the PADIE model to make a smooth transition into the new way of doing business.

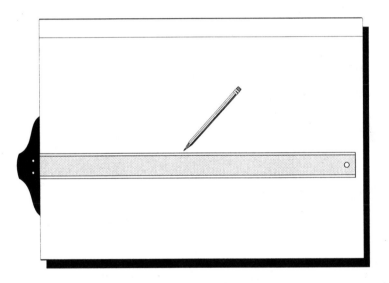

The next five chapters present an in-depth discussion and illustration of each phase in the Team Transition Model. Watch as Prestige Printing puts PADIE into action!

CHAPTER THREE WORKSHEET:
THE TRANSITION MODEL AND YOUR TEAM

1. a) Given the nature of your organization and your team, which of the five phases of transition do you feel will be the most critical to your successful transition to a self-managed team?

_____

_____

b) Why?

_____

_____

2. a) Which do you feel will be the most challenging phase?

_____

_____

_____

b) Why?

_____

_____

_____

_____

3. a) Which phase do you feel will present the least difficulty?

_____

_____

_____

b) Why?

_____

_____

_____

4. What support do you feel you'll need to make a successful transition to a self-managed team?

a) From the team itself?

_____

_____

_____

b) From outside the team?

_____

_____

_____

_____

PHASE ONE: PLAN

Proper planning is vital to the success of any project. Your work group should take the necessary time to plan before you make the transition to a self-managed team.

The Plan phase involves three main steps:

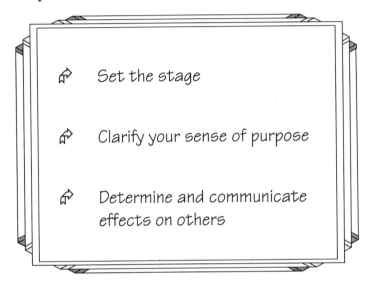

☞   Set the stage

☞   Clarify your sense of purpose

☞   Determine and communicate effects on others

Remember, a little time spent now can save you from running into unexpected trouble later.

Set The Stage

Your first action is to clarify why there is to be a changeover to a self-managed team. Make sure everyone understands why your organization or work group needs to change to this new way of doing business (*i.e., to improve work performance and increase customer satisfaction*). After all, the goal of your planning process is to make a successful transition to a self-managed team. And a successful transition requires clear understanding.

Note: This decision to make the transition to self-managed teams does not necessarily mean that any employee has been doing a poor job.

Ultimately, the main reason an organization chooses to reorganize into self-managed teams is to increase customer satisfaction. In self-managed teams employees will address customer concerns quickly rather than waiting for management to act. Faster delivery of quality products and services leads to higher customer satisfaction. That means repeat business, more job satisfaction, and customer retention.

Let's see how the Prep Department is doing . . .

Bob, the Prep Department manager, called a team meeting. He opened with a brief presentation explaining what self-managed teams are and why Prestige chose this approach.

"You probably remember the point our owner, Mr. Allison, made at our all-employee meeting last month. He said we should all think of ourselves as the Chief Executive Officers of our own work areas. He also talked about operators working in self-managed teams as another example of how this company gives everyone the opportunity to grow and contribute."

"Self-managed teams will do all the things that supervisors do now, in fact there will not even be a job called supervisor," Bob said. He told the group that everyone's job would change, even his own.

"Well, we're ready to start, with the Prep Department as a pilot team. We believe this approach will benefit each of us, the company, and most importantly, our customers."

"Each of the teams will report to my boss, Ann, the Vice President of Operations. Eventually, the whole company will be organized into self-managed teams and all will report directly to a member of senior management." Bob said he would help guide the Prep Department teams through the pilot stage. He would then move on to facilitate another department's changeover to self-managed teams.

The way Bob accepted the change to his own job made everyone feel more at ease. The employees still had concerns, but after much discussion everyone seemed willing to give it a try. . . .

Clarify Your Sense Of Purpose

The next step in establishing a self-managed team is to define your group identity. This means developing a *vision*, a *mission*, and *core values*. A vision is a picture in your mind of an optimistic future for your team. Creating a team vision involves group brainstorming and discussion of questions like these :

➡ What would it be like if all the problems and obstacles were removed from our jobs?

➡ What do we as a team want to become in the future?

➡ How do we want others to view our work group?

➡ What do we want our customers to say about us?

Spend time discussing the answers to these questions. Make sure everyone participates and offers their ideas. It may be difficult for some people to imagine a workplace without the problems, hassles and headaches that they experience on a regular basis.

Encourage people to be optimistic. While the team discusses ideas, write them on a flip chart or whiteboard. It may take you some time to arrive at the statement that accurately expresses the future your team wants to create.

Bob continued the meeting . . .

with a discussion about group identity. He asked everyone to visualize an optimistic future for the department. The staff spent 20 minutes discussing ideas. After struggling for the right words, they had an initial vision statement. It read:

Our Vision

To be respected and appreciated by our customers, both internal and external, for the outstanding quality of our work, the quickness of our turn-around times, our flexibility, and our attentiveness.

Mission

After completing a vision statement, put together a mission statement. Your mission is a statement of purpose, or what your team does and must do to achieve its vision. It describes the unique value your team contributes to the organization.

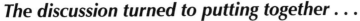

The discussion turned to putting together . . .

a mission statement. Bob explained the mission as *"the reason we are here—a statement of purpose."* After 40 minutes, they had the following mission statement:

> ### Our Mission
>
> Working cooperatively as a unified team, we contribute to the success of Prestige Printing by providing superior film processing, stripping, proofing, and platemaking products and services that meet or exceed customer requirements.

Core Values

Finally, put together a list of core values, or your team's set of guiding principles. Hold a discussion and list team members' responses to these questions:

➡ What do we as a team believe in?

➡ What principles will guide us in working with each other?

➡ What behaviors will help us achieve our vision and carry out our mission?

As with the vision and mission statements, it may take some time before everyone can come to agreement on the core values. It is important to begin making team decisions by consensus.

The Prep Department was still . . .

in the first phase of preparation—planning. They began compiling a list of their core values. Everyone brainstormed a list of possible core values and then reduced them to the following:

Prep Department's Core Values

➡ Customer needs are more important than anything else

➡ Flexibility and "yes we can" is our attitude

➡ We are always open to new ideas

➡ There is always a better way

➡ Information is shared with everyone

The purpose of having a vision, a mission, and core values is to guide members of your team in making the right choices. The right decisions are the ones that move the team toward your vision. By acting according to your core values, your team will continue moving in the right direction.

In the past, members of your team may have waited for instructions. Few employees took action without first getting management approval. This won't work in a self-managed team environment, where you'll need to make your own decisions. Having a clear sense of the team's vision, mission and core values will add certainty and direction to team decision making.

Determine And Communicate Effects On Others

Other groups within the organization need to know what's going on during your planning. You should also inform your team's internal suppliers and customers about the changes being planned. Since your team will be doing business in a new way, other groups may have to coordinate and communicate with your team in a different way.

As a team, list all your internal suppliers (*i.e., those groups within the organization whom you rely on to provide you with products, services or information*). In the past, the group supervisor was the main point of contact with other groups, but within a self-managed team, the employees themselves will be dealing directly with these suppliers.

Your internal customers, those groups who depend upon your team for products and services, should also be prepared for the changes. These internal customers must adjust to working with different members of your team.

Communicate Self-Managed Team Transition Plan

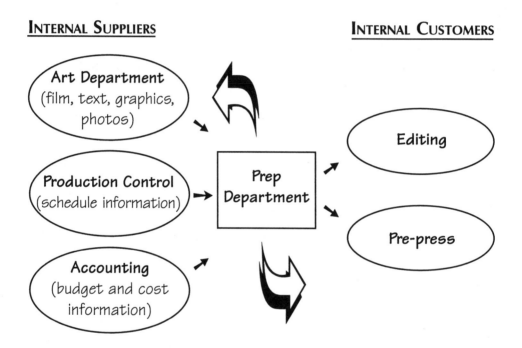

INTERNAL SUPPLIERS   INTERNAL CUSTOMERS

- Art Department (film, text, graphics, photos)
- Production Control (schedule information)
- Accounting (budget and cost information)

Prep Department

- Editing
- Pre-press

Bob continued the meeting . . .

with a discussion about Prep's internal suppliers and customers *(e.g., the Art Department provides film with text, graphics and photographs; Production Control provides schedule information, and Accounting supplies budget and cost information).*

Bob said Ann would meet with all department managers to explain Prestige's plans for implementing self-managed teams. In addition, Bob would write a memo to all employees explaining what to expect from the changeover.

CHAPTER FOUR WORKSHEET:
PLANNING YOUR TRANSITION PROCESS

1. What are the key reasons for your organization/team to transition to a self-managed team environment?

_____

_____

_____

_____

_____

2. What key words, phrases, or points need to be included in your vision?

_____

_____

_____

_____

_____

_____

3. What are the key words, phrases, or points that need to be included in your mission?

_____

_____

_____

_____

_____

_____

4. What core values (*four to six*) are critical to your success as a self-managed team?

_____

_____

_____

_____

_____

_____

_____

_____

_____

5. (a) What will be the effect on and how will you involve your
   internal suppliers?

_____

_____

_____

_____

_____

_____

_____

(b) Your internal customers?

_____

_____

_____

_____

_____

_____

_____

PHASE TWO: ANALYZE

The next phase of the PADIE model is Analyze. Here you will analyze how ready you are to make the transition to a self-managed team. The Analyze phase involves four main steps:

☞ Clarify team management responsibilities

☞ Determine the work responsibilities and cross-training needed

☞ See that everyone has the right attitude to succeed

☞ Clarify the policies and procedures that need to be changed

Since members will learn multiple job functions, you will need to assess the skills of each member of your team. You should also analyze procedures to determine what changes are necessary.

Clarify Team Management Responsibilities

Self-managed teams do not have supervisors. Instead, all team members share the responsibility for handling the management tasks. The first thing you need to do is clarify what a supervisor does all day.

With the team members, list on a flip chart or whiteboard all of the things supervisors do. It is important for team members to realize the additional responsibilities associated with being a member of a self-managed team.

Many of these responsibilities *(e.g., hiring, pay issues, and discipline problems)* are best handled during a team meeting. In addition, individuals should do other tasks such as ordering supplies and coordinating with other work groups. During the team meeting, members can volunteer to take care of these responsibilities as needed.

Management Responsibilities

Schedule work flow

Hire temps

Order supplies

Handle discipline problems

The next Monday morning, the Prep Department . . .

gathered for another meeting. Bob said the purpose of the meeting *"was to analyze what we need to do to manage ourselves as a team."* They began by listing on the large whiteboard each of the management tasks necessary to run the Prep Department. The supervisors took turns describing the jobs in their groups and what types of skills were needed to do them. This led to a discussion of learning multiple jobs and cross-training. . . .

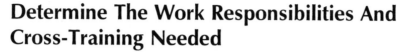

Determine The Work Responsibilities And Cross-Training Needed

Members of self-managed teams learn to do many different jobs and become multiskilled. This adds flexibility to your current methods of producing products and delivering services. Multiskilled people can cover for each other, and rotate from job to job as needed. The first step is to analyze the skills everyone has and then determine who has the potential to learn new jobs.

Bob next drew a large matrix . . .

on the whiteboard. He listed every team member's name vertically down the left side and each position in the department horizontally across the top. He had everyone identify the job(s) they were doing and those jobs they had the skills to learn. . . .

Job Skills Matrix—Prep Department

NAME	CAMERA OPERATOR	SCANNER OPERATOR	STRIP SPECIALIST	PROOFER	PLATE MAKER
Greg	X	O	X	O	
James	O		X	X	O
Teri	X		O	O	X
Noriko	X		X	X	O
Quan		X	O		X
O = already knows this job X = has the skills to learn this job					

Use the matrix to analyze cross-training needs and opportunities. Later, when you form your self-managed team, everyone will learn another job from a fellow team member, while teaching someone else to do their job.

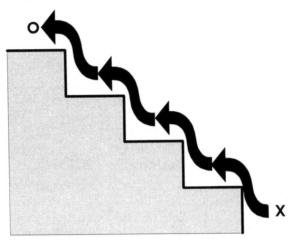

See That Everyone Has The Right Attitude To Succeed

It's a good idea to spend a few minutes making sure everyone involved has the right attitude to make the change work. Discuss the following questions:

➠ What concerns do you have about forming self-managed teams?

➠ What do you see as the benefits?

➠ What do you see as potential problems?

➠ What will you lose?

➠ What will you gain?

Some people in the Prep Department . . .

felt very confident about their ability to learn many new jobs. Others had been doing the same job for so long that they didn't have much faith in their ability to do anything else. It wasn't easy to decide which jobs a person could learn because no one understood each job fully yet.

Holding discussions about attitudes gives you the opportunity to address concerns, dispel rumors, and put people at ease.

Clarify The Policies And Procedures That Need To Be Changed

The implementation of self-managed teams means many of the policies and procedures currently in place will change. This is because they are oriented toward a structure with several levels of management. You should authorize team members to do what your policy manual currently permits only management to do.

LEVELS OF MANAGEMENT

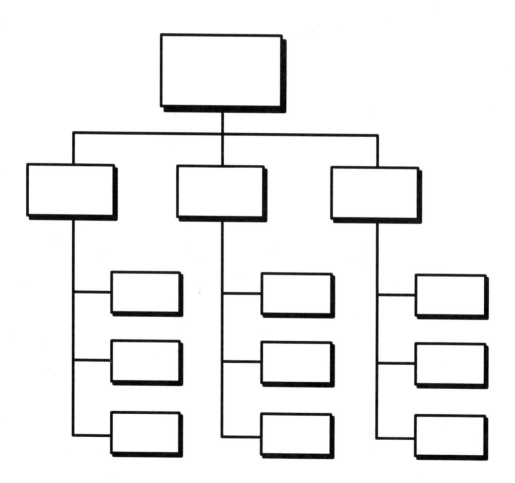

Items in your policies and procedures manual that need to be changed may include:

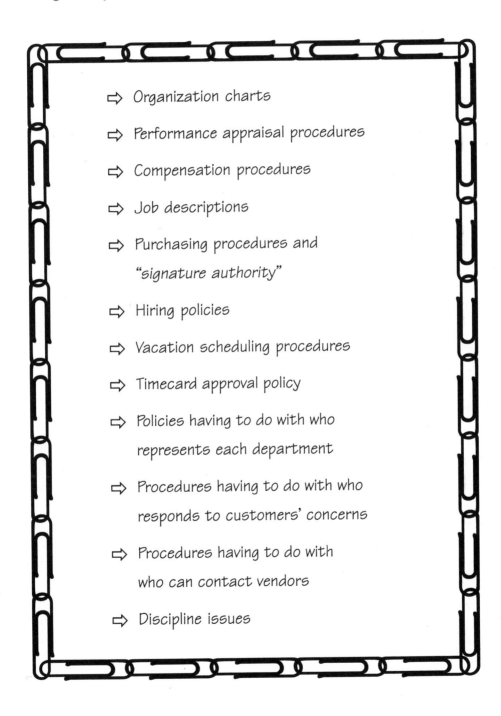

⇨ Organization charts

⇨ Performance appraisal procedures

⇨ Compensation procedures

⇨ Job descriptions

⇨ Purchasing procedures and "signature authority"

⇨ Hiring policies

⇨ Vacation scheduling procedures

⇨ Timecard approval policy

⇨ Policies having to do with who represents each department

⇨ Procedures having to do with who responds to customers' concerns

⇨ Procedures having to do with who can contact vendors

⇨ Discipline issues

CHAPTER FIVE WORKSHEET: ANALYZING YOUR TEAM'S READINESS

1. What are the specific management responsibilities that the team has to assume?

- _____   - _____
- _____   - _____
- _____   - _____
- _____   - _____
- _____   - _____

2. Identify which team members are currently prepared to handle the various work responsibilities, and what the cross-training needs are.

Name	Job, Task, or Position _____	Job, Task, or Position _____

O = already knows this job, task, or position   X = has the skills to learn

3. What specific concerns, problems, and issues do you and other team members foresee as you move toward self-managed teams?

_____

_____

_____

_____

_____

_____

4. What specific policies and procedures need to be revised as part of the transition?

_____

_____

_____

_____

_____

_____

_____

PHASE THREE: DESIGN

The next step in the PADIE model is Design. Using the results of the Analyze phase, you will now decide how to design the team to best meet your customers' needs and expectations.

The Design phase involves four main steps:

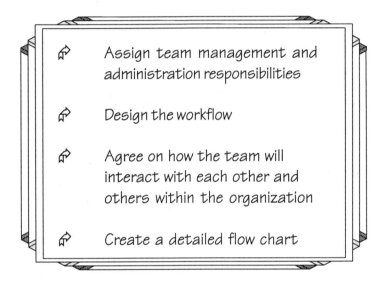

> Assign team management and administration responsibilities

> Design the workflow

> Agree on how the team will interact with each other and others within the organization

> Create a detailed flow chart

Assign Team Management And Administration Responsibilities

Look at the types of work being done by your group and the types of customers you serve. You should organize self-managed teams that focus on a certain type of product or service output.

Consider:

➡ what tasks your group performs and who does them

➡ how many self-managed teams to form and whom to assign to them

➡ who should fill specific roles and responsibilities

The Design phase is also where you put together a cross-training plan. One option is to pair people up and locate their work areas close together. Build time for cross-training into the daily work schedule.

Prep Department - SMT Transition Schedule

NAME	MON. AM	MON. PM	TUES. AM	TUES. PM	WED. AM	WED. PM	THURS. AM	THURS. PM	FRI. AM	FRI. PM
Greg			Cross-Train					Cross-Train		
James				Cross-Train					Cross-Train	
Teri		Cross-Train								
Noriko								Cross-Train		
Quan					Cross-Train					

Balance is the key here. Your group must find a balance between cross-training each other and doing necessary work. Learning new skills must not become so important that customer satisfaction is threatened by not meeting current customer needs.

Each team also decides how to handle responsibilities previously managed by supervisors. In the Design phase, you determine which tasks will be decided by team consensus and which can be handled by a single team member.

SAMPLE: PREP DEPARTMENT RESPONSIBILITIES MATRIX	
TASK	WHO IS RESPONSIBLE?
Scheduling	Team
Job assignments	Team
Training	Team
Quality standards	Team
Costs and budgets	Greg and Quan
Interviewing and hiring	Team
Performance reviews	Team
Coordination with other areas	James and Teri

Bob and the rest . . .

of the Prep Department transition team decided to first assign the responsibilities. They were surprised when they finished their list that so many of
their responsibilities were assigned to the team itself, instead of to individual
members . . . .

One person may handle some of these responsibilities, such as
reviewing timecards, but even they should be rotated every two to
three months.

Design The Work Flow

You should also consider how the tasks in each work process will flow from one person to the next. You can avoid bottlenecks by making sure the right people and equipment are assigned to each job.

Avoid Bottlenecks in Management

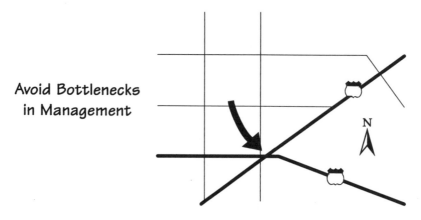

It's a good idea to flow chart the new process task. A flow chart is like a large map. It shows your team how all the steps fit together. It allows people to agree or disagree with the sequence of tasks. It also allows you to draw *"the way it is now,"* analyze it for problems, and then draw *"the way it should be."*

Prep Department Transition Team
Work Flow: Web Fed Jobs

Camera Work → Scanning → Stripping → Proofing → Plate Making

Other Points To Consider

➠ Think about how much space each team will need.

➠ Do you have adequate equipment?

➠ Will each team have their own equipment or will teams share certain items?

➠ Agree on a work area for each team.

➠ Consider where to locate each person's work station.

Prep was laid out according to groups . . .

Each group had their own work area; some members had their own cubicles, some had drafting tables, and the supervisors had private offices. This would all change.

Bob presented the plan to organize self-managed teams according to the types of printing job the customers wanted. Since Prestige did all types of printing jobs, the idea was to form teams that specialized in a certain type of printing work. They would move equipment to fit the best work flow. Bob asked that no one get too attached to any turf. . . .

Agree On How The Team Will Interact

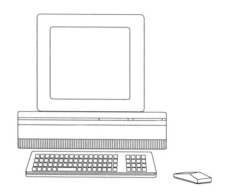

In the Design phase, you will also establish the details of team meetings and other methods of team communication. Will the team meet every day and/or communicate electronically via a computer network? Plan to allow plenty of time for team meetings, at least for the first six months.

Team coordinator

Once you figure out who is on which team, discuss the team coordinator role. The coordinator is *not* a substitute for the supervisor. She or he is no different from any other team member. Team members often vote for the team coordinator, who serves for eight to twelve weeks *(or more, depending on the nature of the team)*, and then the responsibility rotates to another member. The coordinator has the most contact with upper management.

Representing the team

The team coordinator and/or assigned members of the team are responsible for attending other types of meetings as the team's representative. However, the coordinator is primarily a working member of the team.

Special problems

During the Design phase, team members should get to know the senior manager to whom their team reports. Team members will turn to this person when they run into special problems that they cannot solve themselves.

Code of Conduct

The next step is establishing a team meeting *"Code of Conduct,"* or a set of rules for getting along with each other. Disagreements often occur during team meetings, which is normal. By reminding each other of the *"Code of Conduct,"* team members will be able to make the best use of their meeting time.

A team meeting Code of Conduct might look like this:

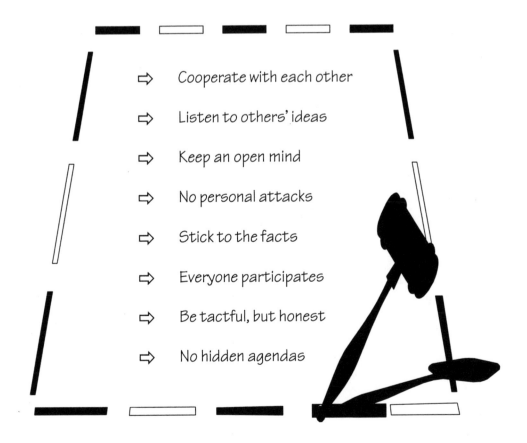

⇨ Cooperate with each other

⇨ Listen to others' ideas

⇨ Keep an open mind

⇨ No personal attacks

⇨ Stick to the facts

⇨ Everyone participates

⇨ Be tactful, but honest

⇨ No hidden agendas

While progressing through the Design phase . . .

Bob took the lead saying, *"We need to decide how we will divide our responsibilities."* He asked the group to discuss the types of printing common to Prestige.

Because Prestige is an *"offset"* print shop with two different types of print work (*i.e., "web fed" and "sheet fed"*), it made sense for the employees to divide into two teams.

At this point, they referred back to the skills matrix they created in the Analyze phase.

For maximum efficiency, each team must include members capable of doing all five jobs (*i.e., scanner operator, camera operator, strip specialist, proofer, and plate maker*). In the future, when members are cross-trained in multiple skills, forming teams will be easier. But now everyone is really only an expert in one skill, so dividing the employees in just the right way is important. . . .

Initial Responsibilities

POSITION	WEB FED TEAM	SHEET FED TEAM
Camera Operators	James	Susan
Scanner Operators	Noriko Greg	Jamal Alex
Strip Specialists	Quan Teri	Yvonne Carmen
Proofers	Greg Teri	Ted Cora
Plate Makers	James Noriko	Fernando Mike

The next step was to . . .

finalize a cross-training plan. Using the matrix they put together in the Analyze phase, each team came up with a partner system for cross-training one another. Team members would spend one hour every other day with their partners, observing how they did their job, asking questions, and assisting them. The next day their partner would spend an hour learning from them. . . .

Prep Department Transition Team
Cross-Training Plan

TEAM MEMBER	CURRENT JOB	PARTNER	CROSS-TRAINED JOB	TEAM
Greg	Scanner	Quan	Strip	Web Fed
Quan	Strip	Greg	Scanner	Web Fed
James	Camera	Teri	Proofer	Web Fed
Teri	Proofer	James	Camera	Web Fed
Teri	Strip	James	Plate	Web Fed
James	Plate	Teri	Strip	Web Fed
Quan	Strip	Noriko	Plate	Web Fed
Noriko	Plate	Quan	Strip	Web Fed

Create A Detailed Flow Chart

Next, you should make a large flow chart showing all the major tasks in a process—from the point the customer places an order until delivery of the product or service.

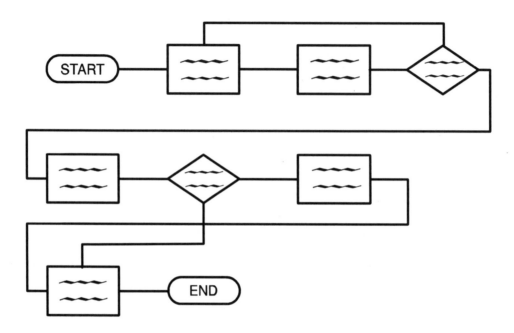

The team gathered again . . .

to plan the new layout of their work area and the assignment of equipment to each team. Bob directed, *"I'd like each of your teams to make a flow chart showing the sequence of tasks we will have to handle in the Prep Department."*

Next, they took an inventory of all the equipment in the department and determined what each team would need.

By the end of the second Design meeting, each team had a plan for their work flow. Bob announced that at the next meeting each team would meet in a separate conference room.

CHAPTER SIX WORKSHEET:
DESIGNING YOUR SELF-MANAGED TEAM

1. To whom will each of the team management and administrative responsibilities be assigned?

_____

_____

_____

_____

_____

_____

2. What are the steps or tasks that the team needs to accomplish to meet or exceed the needs of its customers *(internal or external)*?

_____

_____

_____

_____

_____

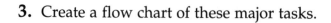
3. Create a flow chart of these major tasks.

Note: Please refer to the guidebook *Continuous Improvement Tools Volume 2* for detailed instructions on creating flowcharts.

4. What specific operating rules or *"Codes of Conduct"* will the self-managed team need?

_____

_____

_____

_____

_____

_____

_____

_____

_____

_____

_____

_____

_____

_____

_____

_____

_____

5. a) What are the responsibilities of the team coordinator?

_____

_____

_____

_____

b) For how long?

_____

_____

_____

c) Who will it be initially?

_____

_____

_____

d) Who will be next?

_____

_____

_____

6. Who will have the primary responsibility for the tasks identified in Question # 2? Who will be cross-trained, by whom, and when?

Transition Team
Cross-Training Plan

TEAM MEMBER	CURRENT JOB	PARTNER	CROSS-TRAINED JOB	TEAM

PHASE FOUR: IMPLEMENT

It's time to implement your team's plans. During this phase, you will begin to operate as a self-managed team. You now have your self-managed teams formed and jobs assigned. You should start handling the details of day-to-day projects as a self-managed team.

The Implement phase involves three main steps:

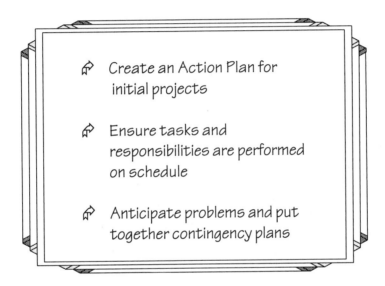

☞ Create an Action Plan for
   initial projects

☞ Ensure tasks and
   responsibilities are performed
   on schedule

☞ Anticipate problems and put
   together contingency plans

Create An Action Plan For Initial Projects

The purpose of an Action Plan is to clarify the responsibilities, time schedules, and costs of each project. If every team member understands the Action Plan, then they know who should do what, in which order, by when, and how much it should cost.

Using an Action Plan ensures accountability by removing uncertainty. Since your whole team is involved in putting the plan together, everyone is clear about their duties.

The first step in creating an Action Plan is to break down a project into smaller chunks by using a flow chart. The project involves a customer work order. Keep in mind that team members must do all tasks, including those formerly done by a supervisor (*e.g., estimating the hours to run a job, ordering supplies, or reviewing the accuracy of timecards*). Be sure to include these tasks on your Action Plan.

In the Web Fed team, James . . .

announced, "*This week we need to start setting up for two big jobs, both of which we've done before. The City Parks and Recreation (CPR) bureau has ordered 125,000 copies of their winter schedule of activities. The front office promised a turnaround date of Wednesday, October 11.*"

"*We also have to run off our usual 3,000 copies of the 'Leisure Village Reporter' (LVR) monthly newsletter,*" he continued. "*Sales promised a delivery date of Monday, October 2. We need to put together an Action Plan to make sure everything goes smoothly with these jobs.*"

The Web Fed team divided each project into separate tasks. Because team members would be cross-training each other, they took into account learning opportunities when they assigned responsibilities. . . .

⟹ Pull supplies from inventory, or order if needed
⟹ Contact customers
⟹ Prepare film
⟹ Scan
⟹ Align negatives
⟹ Strip
⟹ Make proof
⟹ Get customer approval
⟹ Make customer-requested changes
⟹ Make plates

Your team most likely will need information from other employees within your organization (*e.g., Accounting may provide cost information and labor hour standards; Production Control can tell you how much work is scheduled in coming months*). Seek out these people's input when you are doing action planning.

> ### Scheduling the CPR and LVR jobs was a challenge . . .
>
> for the team. On the one hand, the CPR job was much larger and more time-consuming, but the LVR job was due almost two weeks earlier. And the only way the team was going to achieve its mission was to satisfy both customers. . . .

After working for one hour, the team had an Action Plan for both customer orders.

Prep Dept. Self-Managed Team's CPR & LVR Action Plan

ACTION STEP TASK/ACTIVITY	RESPONSIBLE PERSONS/GROUP	BEGIN DATE	END DATE	ESTIMATED HOURS	COST
1. Pull supplies from inventory or order as needed (LVR)	Greg/Teri	9/18	9/18	1.5	$365
2. Contact (LVR)	James/Quan	9/18	9/18	3	$48
3. Contact (CPR)	James/Quan	9/18	9/18	4	$62
4. Prepare film (LVR)	Greg/Noriko	9/19	9/19	4	$72
5. Etc.					

LVR—Leisure Village Reporter job   CPR—City Parks and Recreation job

The team members were assigned to each task in cross-training pairs. The person with the primary expertise in each task had the chief responsibility. Each cross-training partner would be available to assist, but he would be mainly concerned with learning the job.

Ensure Tasks And Responsibilities Are Performed On Schedule

Once your team has put together an Action Plan to fulfill a customer order, you need a way to track your progress. Each action step has a beginning and ending date with an estimated number of hours to complete each activity. Your team does not need to monitor each activity to make sure that all work is completed on time and within budget. Instead the team should address only unexpected issues or problems.

If the team runs into snags, discuss the problem. In this way, team members can pool their experience and common sense to solve problems and remove obstacles.

Your team may find it helpful to use charts or graphs to visually display information such as cost, schedule, and quality ratings. Post large, *"visual"* charts in your work area so everyone can get feedback on how they are doing.

At one of the morning team meetings . . .

James had included the subject of measurements on the agenda. How did they know how they were performing? After some discussion, the team decided to track the actual time to complete each task and compare it with the estimated time. Everyone was in agreement that the time estimates were not accurate. Tracking how long it actually took to complete each item on the Action Plan would help the team improve the next Action Plan. . . .

Anticipate Problems And Put Together Contingency Plans

Sometimes even the best plans may run into problems. For this reason, it is important to do contingency planning. A contingency plan is a backup or *"just-in-case"* plan. If you should experience an unplanned problem, your whole team wouldn't have to stop and try to figure out what to do. It isn't possible to think through every possibility, but your team is likely to anticipate the most obvious ones.

When creating a contingency plan with your team, discuss your Action Plan and the following questions:

➡ What potential problems could occur at each action step?

➡ How will we deal with them if they occur?

➡ What can we do to *"head off"* potential problems?

Step-By-Step Problem Solving

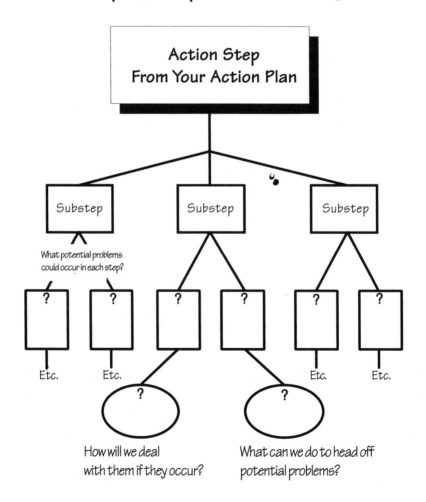

On Thursday, Bob attended the . . .

Web Fed team meeting. He only stayed briefly, just long enough to get the team members to begin thinking about contingency plans. *"I've looked over your Action Plan,"* Bob said, *"and my only feedback to you would be to think about contingencies. The way you have things scheduled assumes that nothing will go wrong."*

The biggest concern for the Web Fed team regarding a backup plan was that certain jobs had only one expert. Greg was the only scanner operator and James was the only camera operator. Greg could learn quickly how to cover the camera work if James was out sick. But then who would cover the scanner work? If Greg was ever sick or took a vacation day, no one would be prepared to use the scanner. This situation needed a contingency plan. . . .

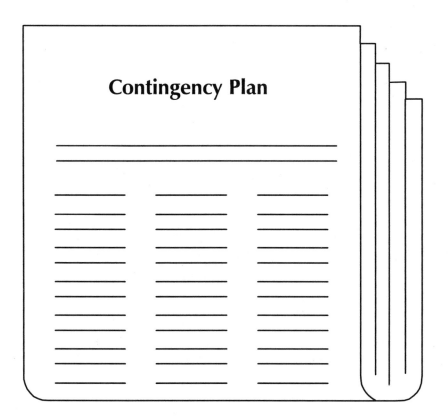

CHAPTER SEVEN WORKSHEET:
IMPLEMENTING YOUR SELF-MANAGED TEAM

1. As a team, develop an Action Plan for one of the first projects
you will handle as a self-managed team.

Action Step Task/Activity	Responsible Persons/Group	Begin Date	End Date	Estimated Hours	Cost
1.					
2.					
3.					
4.					
5.					

2. a) How will your team monitor its progress in the early stages
of operating as a self-managed team?

_____

_____

_____

_____

b) Will this monitoring process be any different after the team has been operating as a self-managed team for some time?

_____

_____

_____

c) How?

_____

_____

_____

_____

3. What specific contingencies will your team plan for the initial Action Plan?

_____

_____

_____

_____

_____

_____

PHASE FIVE: EVALUATE

Once your self-managed team is formed and operating, you need a way to stay on track. The Evaluate phase is where you do a *"reality check"* on how the team is performing. Your team will need to pay attention to the opinions and comments of your customers, both inside and outside the organization. It is important to *"build in"* ways to monitor or evaluate the results of your self-managed team. This is important to gain quick feedback about a problem and take action to eliminate the causes.

The Evaluate phase involves three main steps:

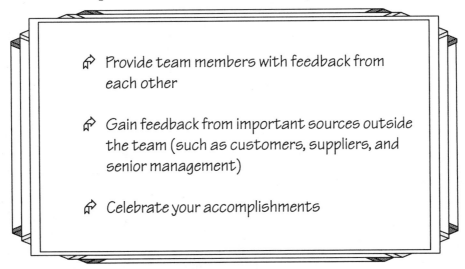

☞ Provide team members with feedback from each other

☞ Gain feedback from important sources outside the team (such as customers, suppliers, and senior management)

☞ Celebrate your accomplishments

Provide Team Members With Feedback From Each Other

To best enable your self-managed team to work well together, you must provide team members the opportunity to give each other feedback. Team members will be working closely with each other, and will be spending time together in meetings. In both of these situations, conflicts are inevitable. Feedback tools will help manage and minimize conflict.

Feedback at team meetings

Conducting effective team meetings is one of the most important aspects of success for any self-managed team. To make sure that team meetings are working well and making the best use of time, team members should regularly evaluate their meetings.

A meeting evaluation consists of reserving time at the end of the meeting to discuss how your team did. During one of the first few team meetings, you should establish a team *"Code of Conduct."* Using the following list of questions, have members review the meeting.

⇨ Was there an agenda?

⇨ Did we stick to the topics listed on the agenda?

⇨ Did the meeting start and end on time?

⇨ Was everyone adequately prepared for the meeting?

⇨ Were decisions timely?

⇨ Did we discuss all the facts before making each decision?

⇨ Was the meeting organized and under control?

⇨ Did we make good use of our time?

⇨ Did everyone participate in the discussion?

⇨ Were action items assigned and followed-up?

⇨ Were meeting minutes recorded and given to everyone?

It was the third week...

since the Prep Department had formed self-managed teams. Each morning, the teams held a brief meeting at the start and end of each shift. Susan, the elected coordinator of the Sheet Fed Team, made up an agenda for each meeting. She was concerned that topics on her agenda were not always covered during meetings and some had to be shelved until the next meeting. She believed that the team should be getting more accomplished during team meetings.

Susan decided to try doing a *"meeting evaluation"* every other day. Most of the team agreed that they were not making the best use of their time. After about ten minutes of discussion, the Sheet Fed team created a list of *"meeting improvement action items."* . . .

- Stick to the topics on the agenda—don't get off-track

- Keep the meeting organized and under control—only one person speaks at a time

- Move through the agenda quickly—make good use of our time

- Balance the discussion—don't let anyone dominate the conversation—draw out the more quiet team members

Invite team members to pick the three or four questions that best apply to the meeting just held. Briefly discuss *"what we did right and should continue doing"* and *"what needs to change and what we should stop doing."* Spending only five minutes at the end of each meeting will remind each member of the proper behavior needed for effective team meetings.

Peer performance feedback

Peer performance reviews are another aspect of the Evaluation phase. Since self-managed team members rely heavily on each other to do their jobs, it makes sense for members to rate each others' work performance. Aspects such as quality of work, amount and speed of work, cooperation, and attendance should be rated by peers once every three months. Honest feedback from your peers lets you know how you are letting them down, and in what ways you need to improve.

The self-managed teams in the Prep Department . . .

had another concern. Over on the Web Fed team, three team members approached James about a teamwork problem. James decided to speak with Ann about it. Ann suggested that he do a *"teamwork assessment,"* gaining the opinions of all members, and then discussing the results at the next team meeting. James agreed and distributed an anonymous questionnaire to his team members.

The following morning Ann attended the Web Fed team meeting. James presented the results of the teamwork assessment. The items with below average scores were:

> ⇨ Does our team spend enough time cross-training each other?
>
> ⇨ Do team members show commitment to working as a self-managed team?
>
> ⇨ Do team members discuss problems openly and honestly?
>
> ⇨ Do team members solve problems together?
>
> ⇨ Are team members able to give each other feedback without starting conflict?

The Web Fed team . . .

spent the next 20 minutes discussing the low ratings. From the discussion, everyone began to understand what was happening. As the cross-training partners began learning each others' jobs, more experienced team members would lose patience with their less experienced partners and just finish the job themselves. This caused anger, frustration, and conflict within the teams. As a result of the difficulties in learning new jobs, some members have the desire to go back to the way things used to be.

From this discussion on teamwork assessment, the members put together a plan to approach cross-training differently. They agreed to spend more time each day on cross-training. They also agreed to stretch out the cross-training rotation schedule, which would give everyone more time to learn the other jobs. When tempers begin to flare, the team members agreed to take a break from the cross-training session for one hour. In one hour, they agreed to try again. The Web Fed team agreed to do another teamwork assessment in one month to compare scores to see if the situation is getting better or getting worse. . . .

"Teamwork" performance feedback

Your self-managed team should assess teamwork at least once each month. Peer reviews should look at the individual members of the team. A teamwork assessment looks at how all the individual members are working together.

The teamwork assessment results should then be used as topics for discussion. If members are honest with each other, they will point out what they see as the predominate weaknesses of the team. Team members should always be looking for ways to improve how the team works together.

Sample Questions For Teamwork Assessment

1	=	Rarely or never	4	=	Fairly often
2	=	Once in a while	5	=	Very frequently
3	=	Sometimes			or always

1. Do we as team members share the responsibilities of leadership and keeping the team on track?

   1 ——— 2 ——— 3 ——— 4 ——— 5

2. Does our team spend enough time cross-training each other?

   1 ——— 2 ——— 3 ——— 4 ——— 5

3. Do team members show commitment to working as a self-managed team?

   1 ——— 2 ——— 3 ——— 4 ——— 5

4. Do team members discuss problems openly and honestly?

   1 ——— 2 ——— 3 ——— 4 ——— 5

5. Do team members spend enough time working to achieve results?

   1 ——— 2 ——— 3 ——— 4 ——— 5

6. Are team members clear about how the team fits in with the rest of the organization?

   1 ——— 2 ——— 3 ——— 4 ——— 5

Gain Feedback From Important Sources Outside The Team

The most important sources of feedback are customers. An internal customer is the department or group that receives and uses the products and services provided by your team. External customers are those who bring work to your organization. They are the end users of the products and services provided by your organization. Only by paying close attention to meeting the needs of your internal customers will you be able to please your external customers.

Internal customer feedback

Your team must seek regular feedback from your internal customers. Perhaps once each month, a representative from your team should meet with an internal customer representative and ask:

⇨ What are your expectations of the products, services, and information that our team provides you?

⇨ Are we meeting your expectations?

⇨ What can we do differently to improve the process?

⇨ Please offer us at least one suggestion so we can better meet your needs.

By listening to your internal customers and responding to their suggestions, your team will become more customer-driven.

One month after forming . . .

their self-managed team, the Sheet Fed members had completed two sizable customer orders. Sunset Yacht Sales had placed an order with Prestige to print their marketing brochure featuring next year's model. Phoenician Galleries had also placed a large order to print their quarterly catalog.

The internal customer of both the Web Fed and Sheet Fed teams is the Press Department, who actually *"runs off"* the quantity ordered and passes them on to the Binding Department. The Sheet Fed team decided to seek feedback from the Press Department on both of the large jobs they prepared since forming self-managed teams.

At first, Elke, one of the supervisors in the Press Department, was surprised that team members were asking how they were doing. They never before took much interest in what Press wanted from them. David, Alex, and Carmen volunteered to interview various members of the Press Department to find out how well the team was meeting their expectations.

During one of Carmen's interviews, she learned that an incomplete work order had caused a problem with the Sunset Yacht Sales job. The Sheet Fed team agreed to fix this problem by making sure all necessary information was on the work order and the details were clarified with Press early in the preparation process.

As a result of these internal customer interviews and the way the Sheet Fed team responded to the feedback, their relationship with the Press Department grew stronger. The team agreed to conduct an internal customer interview within 48 hours after every job was turned over to Press. . . .

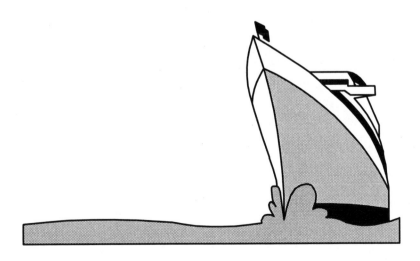

External customer feedback

External customers should be surveyed upon delivery of every order. Typically, your sales department has the most frequent contact with external customers. Therefore, they are in the best position to do follow-up phone calls to determine how pleased customers are with the product or service your organization has provided them. They can ask the same questions you asked your internal customers.

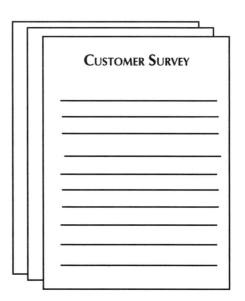

Of course, suggestions for improvements that will lead to better customer satisfaction must be fed back to the team responsible for making the needed changes.

CUSTOMER SURVEY

Internal supplier feedback

You should also seek feedback from the internal suppliers to your team. You must coordinate well with them to satisfy your own internal customers. If your team does not clearly communicate your expectations to them, you cannot expect them to meet your needs. Ask internal suppliers the following questions:

➡ Are you clear about what our team expects from you?

➡ What suggestions do you have to improve the coordination between our groups?

➡ What seems to get in the way of smooth coordination between our groups?

Finally, your self-managed team should also seek regular feedback from the senior manager to whom the team is responsible. Simply ask:

➡ What are we doing right, and what should we continue doing?

➡ What do we need to change or stop doing altogether?

Celebrate Your Accomplishments

Don't underestimate the importance of taking time to celebrate your team's hard work. Plan a team luncheon or get together after work. You'd be surprised how small social events such as these can improve teamwork and morale. Even small expressions of thanks can make lasting impressions upon people.

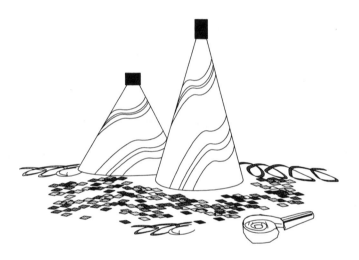

Six weeks after they originally formed . . .

into self-managed teams, Ann decided a celebration was in order. She asked all members of the Prep Department to lunch at a popular restaurant. Prestige would pick up the tab. Bob was also invited as he had played a key role in launching the self-managed teams. During the past few weeks, Bob had been working with the Art Department, getting them prepared to form self-managed teams.

When team members arrived at the restaurant, they were taken to a private room decorated with balloons, confetti, and multicolored streamers. After lunch, Ann passed out a *"Certificate of Appreciation"* to each team member. She told them how pleased Prestige was with their results so far and encouraged them all to continue working together and learning from their experiences.

CHAPTER EIGHT WORKSHEET: EVALUATING YOUR TEAM'S SUCCESS

1. What criteria will you use to evaluate the success of your self-managed team?

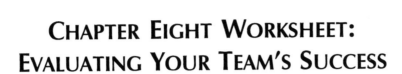

_____

_____

_____

_____

_____

_____

2. What mechanisms, skills, or techniques will team members use to provide each other with feedback?

_____

_____

_____

_____

_____

_____

3. How will feedback be obtained from:

a) Customers

_____

_____

_____

_____

_____

_____

_____

_____

b) Suppliers

_____

_____

_____

_____

_____

_____

_____

_____

4. How will the team celebrate its success?

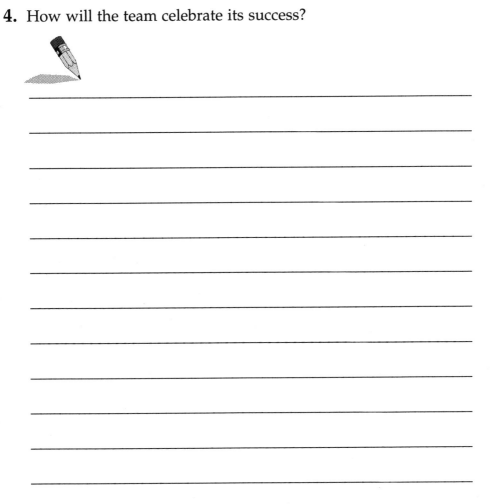

CHAPTER NINE

SUMMARY

You have read about how to get there. You have an idea of what it will be like as a member of a self-managed team once you get there. All that remains is to start the process, if you haven't already. Each of the phases of the PADIE model cover key elements of the transition process.

☑ By **planning** the transition, you will set the stage, clarify your sense of purpose, and let others know about your plan. The most important element of this phase is to make sure everyone understands why the transition is underway. Only then can employees be expected to participate in the transition.

☑ By **analyzing** what has to be done, and what resources your new team will have to work with, you will see what your group has to accomplish to satisfy your internal and external customers. This phase provides focus for the transition.

☑ By **designing** the team around a plan and an analysis of what needs to be done, you will be ensuring the team is maintaining its course on the path to success.

☑ By **implementing** a specific course of action as a team, with solid coordination and communication, the sense of teamwork begins to produce tangible results. The products or services are now provided by a team that manages its own destiny.

☑ By **evaluating** your progress, your self-managed team will truly be on the path to continuous improvement. Your team will define its strengths, respond to its challenges, and celebrate its successes.

Self-Managed Team

Evaluate

Implement

Design

Analyze

Plan

Traditional Work Groups

ONGOING CHALLENGES FOR SELF-MANAGED TEAMS

Your team will continue to face challenges even after working through a successful transition. Each member of your group needs to acquire or refine the following skills to succeed in meeting these challenges as a self-managed team.

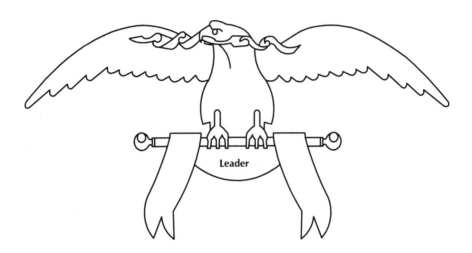

Leadership

Your department manager will lead your group down the road to self-managed teams, but soon the members of your department will need to take over the leadership role. This means they will need leadership skills. Leaders can inspire others to take action and become enthusiastic about what they are doing. They can keep the excitement going and keep the team on track, moving in the right direction. Leadership is not merely a title, it is a shared responsibility. Everyone must be ready to act as a leader whenever the situation requires it.

Communication

At this point, members of your department rely on management to communicate with the rest of the organization. Soon you will be responsible for your own communication and will need to improve your communication skills *(both verbal and written)*. Members will do a lot more face-to-face talking to each other and with people in other departments. Team members will handle all communication that supervisors once did.

Process Improvement

As Prep employees prepared to form self-managed work teams, they found it necessary to learn process-improvement skills. These skills included redesigning the workflow to save time. They used a continuous improvement tool *(flow charting)* to do this.

Your team must also learn to identify and eliminate activities that do not add value to your customer. It is important to understand your customers' needs because their expectations should ultimately drive the work process.

Team Dynamics

After the Prep Department divided into two self-managed teams, members found it necessary to learn team dynamics skills. Sometimes called group dynamics or teamwork, these skills are used on the job and many times during each team meeting. Team dynamics skills help make a meeting effective. They ensure that everyone participates, but no one dominates the discussion. Understanding team dynamics will help a team manage conflict when tempers flare. It will also help keep a meeting on track so that the agenda is covered and the meeting ends on time.

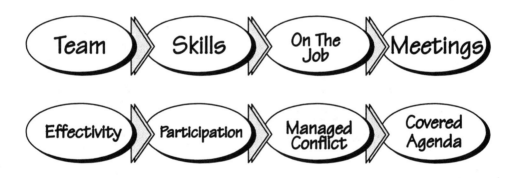

Project Management

To succeed as a self-managed team, members need project management skills. These skills help teams keep their costs under budget and the projects on schedule. The Prep Department used project management skills in creating an Action Plan.

Project management skills may be used when:

➡ A complex customer order must be broken down into manageable chunks

➡ Team members need to accurately estimate the time it will take to finish tasks

➡ A method is required to track the actual time and compare it with the estimated time

➡ The team tries to keep the job under budget

Conflict Management

Success as a self-managed team depends upon team members' ability to handle conflict. Whenever many people share the responsibility for making decisions, differences of opinion can lead to conflict.

It is important to realize that conflict is not necessarily a bad thing. Discussion of opposing views often leads to a better decision.

The key to achieving the best decision is not to allow differing views to damage the spirit of teamwork.

Team members must learn to manage their differences, and to encourage a healthy disagreement without letting conflict destroy cooperation. Successful teams explore differing opinions and work through conflict in a way that allows each member to feel understood and respected.

Consensus Decision Making

Employees must learn to make consensus decisions as a group. Members must be able to discuss their differences and the reasons behind their opinions. Only by really listening to each other's views will members be able to reach a compromise. When members reach a middle ground that everyone can live with, they have achieved a consensus.

Peer Coaching And Feedback

Now that the Prep Department's team members have the responsibility of cross-training each other, peer coaching skills become important. Coaching means guiding someone else to discover the best way of doing something.

Coaching does not involve telling other people what to do. It involves asking them questions and then letting them try to do the task for themselves. When the learner makes mistakes, the coach helps them learn from their experience. When you actually do the task and then learn from the experience, the lessons become more powerful.

Group Problem Solving

The ability to solve problems in a group is necessary to succeed as a self-managed team. Using a structured problem-solving process and various problem-solving tools will help team members find the root cause of a problem. Then you can eliminate the source of the problem so it never appears again. Without using a structured problem-solving process, team problem solving amounts to little more than aimless conversation. Even if the team comes up with a solution, unless they have found the root cause of the problem, it will reappear.

Interpersonal

Succeeding as a self-managed team requires all members to use good interpersonal skills. These skills involve getting along well with other people. To get along effectively, team members must be able to listen, understand, and give feedback without stirring up conflict. The skill of providing feedback, both positive and negative, is the key to correcting poor performance. Only by using proper interpersonal skills will team members be ready to manage themselves well.

REPRODUCIBLE FORMS

JOB SKILLS MATRIX

NAME	JOB, TASK, OR POSITION	JOB, TASK, OR POSITION	JOB, TASK, OR POSITION	JOB, TASK, OR POSITION	JOB, TASK, OR POSITION

O = already knows this job, task, or position   X = has the skills to learn

ADDITIONAL RESOURCES
FROM RICHARD CHANG ASSOCIATES, INC.

Improve your training sessions and seminars with the ideal tools—videos from Richard Chang Associates, Inc. You and your team will easily relate to the portrayals of real-life workplace situations. You can apply our innovative techniques to your own situations for immediate results.

TRAINING VIDEOTAPES

Mastering Change Management*
Turning Obstacles Into Opportunities

Step-By-Step Problem Solving*
A Practical Approach To Solving Problems On The Job

Quality: You Don't Have To Be Sick To Get Better**
Individuals Do Make a Difference

Achieving Results Through Quality Improvement**

*Authored by Dr. Richard Chang and produced by Double Vision Studios.
**Produced by American Media Inc. in conjunction with Richard Chang Associates, Inc.
  Each video includes a Facilitator's Guide.

"THE HUMAN EDGE SERIES" VIDEOTAPES

Total Quality: Myths, Methods, Or Miracles
Featuring Drs. Ken Blanchard and Richard Chang

Empowering The Quality Effort
Featuring Drs. Ken Blanchard and Richard Chang

Produced by Double Vision Studios.

"THE TOTAL QUALITY SERIES"
TRAINING VIDEOTAPES AND WORKBOOKS

Building Commitment *(Telly Award Winner)*
How To Build Greater Commitment To Your TQ Efforts

Teaming Up
How To Successfully Participate On Quality-Improvement Teams

Applied Problem Solving
How To Solve Problems As An Individual Or On A Team

Self-Directed Evaluation
How To Establish Feedback Methods To Self-Monitor Improvements

Authored by Dr. Richard Chang and produced by Double Vision Studios, each videotape from *"The Total Quality Series"* includes a *Facilitator's Guide* and five *Participant Workbooks* with each purchase. Additional *Participant Workbooks* are available for purchase.

EVALUATION AND FEEDBACK FORM

We need your help to continuously improve the quality of the resources provided through the Richard Chang Associates, Inc., Publications Division. We would greatly appreciate your input and suggestions regarding this particular guidebook, as well as future guidebook interests.

Please photocopy this form before completing it, since other readers may use this guidebook. Thank you in advance for your feedback.

Guidebook Title: _____

1. Overall, how would you rate your *level of satisfaction* with this guidebook? Please circle your response.

    Extremely Dissatisfied   Satisfied   Extremely Satisfied

         1   2   3   4   5

2. What specific *concepts or methods* did you find <u>most</u> helpful?

    _____
    _____

3. What specific *concepts or methods* did you find <u>least</u> helpful?

    _____
    _____

4. As an individual who may purchase additional guidebooks in the future, what *characteristics/features/benefits* are most important to you in making a decision to purchase a guidebook *(or another similar book)*?

    _____
    _____

5. What additional *subject matter/topic areas* would you like to see available as a guidebook in the future?

    _____
    _____

Name *(optional):* _____

Address: _____

C/S/Z: _____ **Phone (** **)** _____

PLEASE FAX YOUR RESPONSES TO: (714) 756-0853
OR CALL US AT: 1-800-756-8096